The Siege at Waco

Titles in the *American Disasters* series:

The Exxon Valdez
Tragic Oil Spill
ISBN 0-7660-1058-9

Hurricane Andrew
Nature's Rage
ISBN 0-7660-1057-0

The L.A. Riots
Rage in the City of Angels
ISBN 0-7660-1219-0

The Mighty Midwest Flood
Raging Rivers
ISBN 0-7660-1221-2

The Oklahoma City Bombing
Terror in the Heartland
ISBN 0-7660-1061-9

Plains Outbreak Tornadoes
Killer Twisters
ISBN 0-7660-1059-7

San Francisco Earthquake, 1989
Death and Destruction
ISBN 0-7660-1060-0

TWA Flight 800
Explosion in Midair
ISBN 0-7660-1217-4

The World Trade Center Bombing
Terror in the Towers
ISBN 0-7660-1056-2

The Siege at Waco

Deadly Inferno

Michael D. Cole

AMERICAN DISASTERS

Enslow Publishers, Inc.

40 Industrial Road	PO Box 38
Box 398	Aldershot
Berkeley Heights, NJ 07922	Hants GU12 6BP
USA	UK

http://www.enslow.com

Library of Congress Cataloging-in-Publication Data

Cole, Michael D.
    The siege at Waco: deadly inferno / Michael D. Cole.
      p. cm. — (American disasters)
    Includes bibliographical references and index.
    Summary: Discusses the incident in Waco, Texas, in 1993 involving
David Koresh and the religious group known as the Branch Davidians.
    ISBN 0-7660-1218-2
    1. Waco Branch Davidian Disaster, Tex., 1993—Juvenile literature.
2. Koresh, David, 1959–1993—Juvenile literature. 3. Branch
Davidians—Juvenile literature. [1. Waco Branch Davidian Disaster,
Tex., 1993. 2. Koresh, David, 1959–1993. 3. Branch Davidians.]
I. Title. II. Series.
BP605.B72C65   1999
976.4'284063—dc21   98-35033
                                     CIP
                                     AC

Printed in the United States of America

10 9 8 7 6 5 4 3 2

To Our Readers: We have done our best to make sure all Internet addresses in this
book were active and appropriate when we went to press. However, the author and
the publisher have no control over and assume no liability for the material available
on those Internet sites or on other Web sites they may link to. Any comments or
suggestions can be sent by e-mail to comments@enslow.com or to the address on the
back cover..

Illustration Credits: AP/Wide World Photos, pp. 1, 6, 8, 10, 12, 14, 18, 20, 25,
29, 30, 32, 34, 36, 38, 40, 41, 42.

Cover Illustration: AP/Wide World Photos

Contents

CHAPTER 1

A Sudden Inferno

Outside the city of Waco, Texas, a disaster was taking place. It was April 19, 1993.

Eighty-three members of a religious group called the Branch Davidians were trapped in a fire. It was spreading rapidly through the collection of buildings the Davidians called Mount Carmel. Among the group's members were men, women, and twenty-five children.

"The whole entire building felt warm all at once . . . then a thick black smoke, and the place became dark," said Marjorie Thomas about her ordeal within the burning buildings of the Branch-Davidian religious compound. "I was making my way out of the building," she said, "and my clothes were starting to melt on me."[1]

For the last fifty-one days, the Davidians' compound had been surrounded by a large number of heavily armed federal officers. The officers, members of the Federal Bureau of Investigation (FBI) and the Bureau of Alcohol, Tobacco, and Firearms (ATF), had been urging all members of the Branch Davidians to come out of their buildings.

Some did. However, eighty-three members had refused to leave their compound. They would not desert their leader, David Koresh.

Koresh was an unusual man. He claimed he could explain some of the writings about God in the Bible's Book of Revelations. Under his leadership, the Branch Davidians had amassed a huge supply of illegal weapons, including machine guns and grenade launchers. These illegal weapons were what had brought the federal officers to their door.

When the officers had arrived at the compound fifty-one days earlier, on February 28, 1993, shooting had

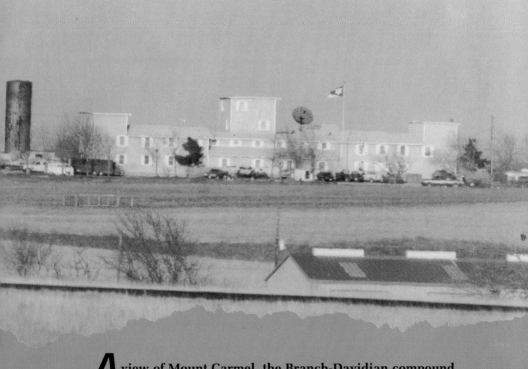

A view of Mount Carmel, the Branch-Davidian compound near Waco, Texas, before the disastrous fire.

broken out. The officers and the Branch Davidians were shooting at each other. After a few hours of exchanged gunfire, neither side was winning, and the incident ended in a standoff, or tie. Four federal officers and two of Koresh's followers were dead.

That evening, after the gunfire, the FBI and the ATF began to negotiate with the Davidians. The negotiations went on and on. During the first two weeks of these talks, a number of the Davidians decided to leave the compound. Further negotiations had gotten nowhere. Now, after six weeks of telephone conversations between the Davidians inside the compound and the FBI agents outside, eighty-three people were still inside Mount Carmel. It did not appear that David Koresh and the people remaining with him would ever come out.

Koresh believed that he and his followers were being forced to take part in a religious war against the forces of evil.

"He has indicated he has been prepared for this confrontation since 1985, that he has stockpiled extensive arms and ammunition," said Bob Ricks, a special agent of the FBI. "He has indicated he would be most pleased if we would engage in a gun-battle with him."[2]

The plan to finally end the fifty-one-day standoff had gone into action that morning, April 19, 1993. At about 6 A.M., FBI negotiators warned Koresh and the Branch Davidians that they would be gassed if they did not come out of the compound immediately. Branch Davidian member Steve Schneider, the main negotiator for Koresh,

Four ATF agents were killed on February 28, 1993, during a gunfight with Branch Davidians. Clockwise from top left: Steve Willis, age 32; Todd McKeehan, age 28; Conway LaBleu, age 30; and Robert Williams, age 26.

responded to the FBI's warning. He hung up the phone and threw it out the window.[3]

Minutes later, two armored vehicles moved slowly toward the compound. They punched holes in the walls. Equipped with special metal tubes, the vehicles pumped a kind of tear gas called CS gas named after its inventors, Ben Carson and Roger Staughton, into the buildings. The FBI and ATF expected the tear gas to force the Branch Davidians out of the buildings through the gaping holes the armored vehicles had made in the walls.

To the agents' surprise, the plan did not work.

The Branch Davidians thought the hole-punching of their walls by the federal agents' armored vehicles was an attack on their compound.

"This is not an assault. This is not an assault," FBI negotiators repeated over the public address loudspeakers. "We will not be entering the building."[4]

Despite the FBI's efforts to assure those inside that they were not under attack, the action of the government's armored vehicles had raised the situation to a crisis level. The Branch Davidians grabbed their weapons and opened fire.

"Leave the building now," the voice on the loudspeaker said. "You are under arrest. This standoff is over."[5]

The armored vehicles backed away, just as they had been ordered to do if they were fired upon. Because the Branch Davidians had opened fire, it was now necessary to use a different type of armored vehicle to continue delivering the tear gas.

*T*he fifty-one-day standoff was exhausting for the authorities, as they waited for something to happen. Terry Newman yawns as he sits on his police car.

Four small tanks, called Bradley fighting vehicles, moved in to deliver the gas in a different way. Using a special port, or opening, in the front of the tanks, they shot small canisters through the compound's windows. The canisters contained the tear gas, which would spread after it was shot inside the buildings.

Over the next few hours, the Bradley vehicles slowly

fired the canisters into the compound. But the winds were high that day. Most of the gas seemed to be blown away by the gusts that swept across the area.

The attempt to drive the group out of the compound with tear gas did not appear to be working. After six hours, no one had come out. But something was indeed happening inside.

At shortly after 12 P.M., flames shot out of the second floor of the compound.

There was a fire!

The flames appeared in three different locations very quickly. The FBI suspected the fire was being set by the Branch Davidians. Earlier that morning, FBI surveillance

*A*n armored vehicle prepares to pound holes into the side of the Branch-Davidian compound in order to shoot canisters of tear gas inside the buildings.

devices, or "bugs," hidden around the compound had revealed Branch-Davidian members saying things like "spread the fuel," and "I want a fire around the back."[6]

Regardless of what had started the fire, the flames spread rapidly. Gusts of wind quickly fanned the blaze through the buildings, trapping those inside.

One of the Branch Davidians heard someone yell, "The fire's been lit! The fire's been lit!"[7]

"Oh my God, they are killing themselves," thought FBI agent Bob Ricks. He watched helplessly as the sudden flames quickly spread over the buildings.[8] The armed Branch Davidians presented a threat to firefighters. Because of this, fire and emergency vehicles had been moved away from the area.

Within moments of the first sign of flames, the fire was wildly out of control. Some of the Branch Davidians were prepared for this moment. A number of them were carrying revolvers or rifles. They were prepared to use them to take their own lives. Others were neither ready nor willing to die.

Marjorie Thomas was one of the many Branch Davidians trying to escape the deadly blaze.

". . . I couldn't see anything. I could hear people moving and screaming, and I still was sitting down while this was happening. Then the voices faded."[9]

As the fire spread, Thomas's friends, including their children, were dying in the spreading smoke and flames. If she did not find a way out very soon, she was sure to die as well. Trying desperately to find a way to escape,

Thomas realized her skin was badly burned by the flames. She was now suffering from third-degree burns over half her body.

"I made my way toward the light, and on doing so, I could see where it—it was one of the bedrooms . . . the window was missing. I looked out."[10]

Thomas had found her way into a bedroom on the second story of the compound. The smoke was thick, and the flames were closing in around her. She had little time before the room would be overcome with fire.

"I don't like heights, but I thought . . . 'I stay inside and die, or I jump out of the window,' so I put my head— my hands over my head and leapt out of the window."[11]

Thomas's leap was successful. She survived her jump from the window, but was badly burned by the fire.

Most others were not so fortunate.

Inside the raging inferno, Koresh's followers were dying from inhaling smoke and being caught under falling debris as they tried to escape. By the time it was over, seventy-four of the Branch Davidians were dead.

Outside, the shocking images of the burning Branch-Davidian compound were carried around the world on live television.

The fifty-one-day standoff between federal officers and the religious group was now ending horribly, in flames. But the sparks that led to the tragic deaths of the Branch Davidians were lighted long before the fiery disaster at Waco.

CHAPTER 2

The Making of David Koresh

The Branch Davidians were created in the 1930s when a group of people broke off, or "branched out," from the Christian Seventh-Day Adventist Church. This new branch opened a commune in Waco, Texas, for "pure Christians." They originally called their group Davidian Seventh-Day Adventists.[1]

The group attracted hundreds of believers. People quit their jobs, sold their belongings, and moved to Waco to await the Second Coming of Jesus Christ. As the years passed, many of these people stopped believing the Davidian preachings and moved away from the Waco compound that was called Mount Carmel.

In the 1970s, a member named Ben Roden took over the group. He changed their name to the Branch Davidians. When Roden died in 1978, the group was left in the control of his widow, Lois, and his son, George.[2]

In 1981, Vernon Howell, who would later call himself David Koresh, came on the scene.

Vernon Howell was born in Houston, Texas, in 1959. He was raised at different times by his mother and his grandparents.

Both his mother and his grandparents were Seventh-Day Adventists. Howell's religious education began early and continued through his teens. He was interested in Bible studies, but he struggled with all systems of formal instruction.

Howell became a carpenter when he moved out on his own at the age of eighteen. It was at about this time that he began to try to influence other people, especially younger boys.

"He really pumped them up," said Howell's girlfriend of that time. "He played with their self-esteem, and they thought it was so neat that here this older guy would take the time to talk to these fourteen- to sixteen-year-olds."[3]

It was only the beginning of his powers to influence others.

After a breakup with his girlfriend, Howell moved to Tyler, Texas. There, he lived with his cousin, and attended the Seventh-Day Adventist Church. At first the church was thrilled to have Howell among its followers. He was a young man who was eager to learn, and he claimed he wished to mend the ways of his sinful past. But soon there were problems.

Howell became very interested in the church's revival meetings. These meetings featured dramatic discussions about the end of the world as foretold in the Bible's Book of Revelations. The more he attended these meetings, the

Vernon Howell (who later changed his name to David Koresh) at age fourteen. His religious upbringing would greatly influence his adult life.

more Howell became convinced that everyone else's theory was wrong.

The Book of Revelations tells of the Seven Seals. These seals close up a scroll that God holds in his right hand. This scroll describes the earthly calamities that will occur before the end of the world. Howell actually believed he might be the person who had the spiritual power to open those Seven Seals. By opening them, Howell believed he would be able to see what the end of the world would be like. In other words, Howell started to believe he was a prophet, like Moses.

The people in the church in Tyler rejected his claim. After Howell stirred up more conflicts at the church, the people there turned him away. Further problems with Howell soon led them to formally reject him from the church. That is when Howell heard of the Branch Davidians at Waco.

The Davidians' current leader, Lois Roden, was in her sixties. The group knew they would need a new leader soon. Howell, with his claims of being a prophet, had arrived at the right time, among a willing group of believers. Before Lois Roden died in 1986, she chose Howell as the group's new leader.

But there was trouble.

In choosing Howell, Lois Roden had passed over her son, George. A dispute broke out between Howell and George Roden, who felt neglected. This dispute resulted in a very bizarre incident.

George Roden went to a cemetery and dug up the

corpse of a Branch-Davidian member. He then challenged that whoever could bring the corpse back to life would be revealed as the true leader of the Branch Davidians.

At this time, Howell was not yet living at the Mount Carmel compound. He and an uncle he had recruited into the Branch Davidians lived together in a local apartment.

Passages from the Bible's Book of Revelations explain the Seven Seals, and how, by the right prophet, they may be opened to reveal how the world will end.

CHAPTER 5

AND I saw in the right hand of him that sat on the throne ᵃa book written within and on the backside, sealed with ᵇseven seals. (2) And I saw a strong angel proclaiming with a loud voice, Who is worthy to open the book, and to loose the seals thereof? (3) And ᶜno man in heaven, nor in earth, neither under the earth, was able to open the book, neither to look thereon.

Because the Branch Davidians made some of their money by buying and selling weapons, some illegally, Howell and his supporters had easy access to guns. On the morning of November 3, 1987, a few days after Roden had dug up the corpse, Howell and seven of his supporters slipped into the compound area. They were armed with assault rifles and carried a camera. Howell later claimed he was sneaking into the compound to take a picture of the corpse. He wanted evidence that could be used to charge Roden with the crime of digging up a dead body. However, Roden surprised the intruders and met Howell and his friends. Roden was armed with a submachine gun. Shooting broke out, and Roden was injured.

Howell and his armed supporters were arrested and put on trial for attempted murder. His supporters were found innocent. The case against Howell was dismissed, after the jury failed to reach a verdict on the charges against him. To his followers, Howell's escape from serious trouble with the authorities seemed almost miraculous.

After the trial, a group of Howell's followers drove a truck to the sheriff's department. They watched with satisfaction as sheriff's deputies loaded it up with dozens of weapons that had been seized from Mount Carmel after the shooting incident on November 3.

"You don't have to stretch your imagination too far to appreciate how his followers interpreted that," said former Branch Davidian Mark Bunds. "He [Howell] had won the verdict, the weapons, and the compound. In his mind, and in those of his people, he must have felt that he was guided by the hand of God."[4]

Howell then moved to Mount Carmel and became the undisputed leader of the Branch Davidians at Waco. Shortly after assuming control, Howell, combining the names of two biblical kings, legally changed his name to David Koresh.

Now using his new name, Koresh transformed the collection of buildings at Mount Carmel into a fortresslike compound. Koresh strongly believed his followers would one day be involved in a war. He greatly expanded the Branch Davidians' arsenal of weapons. He also began training his followers in military tactics. He wanted them to be prepared for the conflict he foresaw in their future.

Members gave their money to the Davidians. The compound also made money by running a nearby auto repair shop, and by trading arms and ammunition. Koresh traveled throughout the southern United States to find new members. He also went to Great Britain and Australia. There he attended religious meetings to draw attention to the message that he was a prophet.

Many people chose to reject his unusual claims. But others did not. Kathryn Schroeder and her husband, Michael, heard Koresh's message through one of his followers. The couple heard about Koresh's claims at a Miami church in 1989. They quickly became fascinated with the Branch-Davidian religion.

The Schroeders packed up their four children and moved to the Branch-Davidian compound at Waco, where they finally met Koresh. However, as soon as the Schroeders arrived at the compound, they learned that marriages were no longer honored.

"All women belonged to David," Kathryn Schroeder later explained. Koresh claimed the scriptures told him that all women at the compound belonged to him, not to their original husbands. Any couples who would remain at the compound had to accept Koresh's strange claim.[5]

Most who lived inside the compound were ready to accept almost everything that David Koresh had to say.

"It's not just that he was enthralling," said former Branch-Davidian member Robert Scott. "It's that everyone else was enthralled, and that made you feel that he must be special, that his message was Divine."[6]

In his final year at the compound, Koresh's behavior became increasingly strange. By late 1992, his followers said his sermons about the end of the world were becoming more and more rambling. Sometimes they were impossible to understand. Koresh told his followers that the government was against them. He often described how they might someday wind up involved in a conflict with the law.

Throughout 1992, Koresh continued to stockpile illegal guns and explosives. He and his followers tested machine guns and set off explosions in areas near the compound. Some of these incidents were witnessed and documented by police. As he continued to buy guns and ammunition illegally, Koresh became convinced that the

Bureau of Alcohol, Tobacco, and Firearms (ATF) was watching the compound. He was correct.

The ATF had secretly been investigating activities around the compound for months. An undercover ATF agent, Robert Rodriguez, had even pretended to become a member of the Branch Davidians in order to spy on the group's illegal activities from inside the compound.

Finally, on the morning of February 28, 1993, an armed force of ATF agents moved toward the compound. They had a warrant to arrest Koresh for illegal possession of firearms and explosive devices. They also had warrants to search the compound for assault rifles, machine guns, grenades, and other weapons.

The ATF was aware of Koresh's unusual religious preachings. Agents feared that simply surrounding the compound and demanding Koresh's surrender might cause the Branch Davidians to fight. Perhaps the Davidians might try to kill the agents, or themselves. Therefore, the ATF agents decided to make a surprise raid on the compound. They picked a time when they hoped the Branch Davidians would not be able to get to their weapons quickly. The agents' strategy failed.

The armed ATF agents and their vehicles had been seen in the Waco area hours before the raid was scheduled to take place. Because of this, the local television station knew that something was about to happen. The station sent a news crew out to the Branch-Davidian compound to cover whatever was going to happen. However, the news crew had difficulty finding the compound. When the cameraman asked someone for directions to the compound, he did not know the person he was asking for directions was Koresh's brother-in-law.

A short time later, Koresh's brother-in-law arrived at the compound. He interrupted a Bible-study session Koresh was leading to warn him that something was about to happen.

Koresh (shown in photo held by Margaret Richardson of Waco) was convinced that ATF agents were watching him, and he began to stockpile even more guns and ammunition.

Robert Rodriguez, the undercover ATF agent, was in attendance at the Branch-Davidian Bible-study session. Koresh had suspected that Rodriguez worked for the ATF, but had tried to recruit him anyway. As soon as Koresh was informed about the raid, he dropped his Bible and said, "Neither the ATF team nor the National Guard will ever get me. They got me once [after the corpse incident] and they'll never get me again."

The study session broke up and the Branch Davidians started preparing for the possible assault by the ATF. Koresh then turned to the window. Without looking at Rodriguez, he said, "They're coming, Robert. The time has come."[7]

Rodriguez immediately made an excuse to leave the compound. As Rodriguez went out the door, Koresh grabbed his hand.

"Good luck, Robert," Koresh said.[8]

Rodriguez left the compound and, within minutes, informed the ATF that Koresh already knew about the raid. Despite the warning from Rodriguez, the ATF agents in command of the raid believed it could still be successful if they raided within the hour.

They were wrong.

The ATF's decision to go ahead with the raid would prove to be a deadly mistake.

CHAPTER 3

The Siege

On the morning of February 28, 1993, less than an hour after Rodriguez had informed the ATF agents that Koresh knew the raid was coming, the ATF force drove up to the compound. Armed agents jumped from their vehicles. Koresh met them just outside the compound's door.

"One of our guys said, '[We're] Federal agents—put your hands up!'" an ATF agent said. "Koresh smiled, backed up and slammed the door. Almost immediately, within seconds, we were ambushed."[1]

"[We] came under heavy and sustained firepower for over half an hour," said ATF agent John Killorin. "We were literally trying to move into position when they opened fire."

Koresh told a different story. He claimed that the ATF agents had fired first.

"They started firing at me," he said. "I fell back in the doorway and we started firing back at them."[2]

Koresh called 911. He was eventually put in phone

contact with the ATF agents, and negotiated a ceasefire. Talks between Koresh and the ATF began. Over the next several days, Koresh allowed a number of women and children to leave the compound. The FBI was also called in, taking part in the negotiations with Koresh. During the ensuing fifty-one-day standoff, a total of thirty-five men, women, and children were released.

The first days of the standoff were grim ones for Kathryn Schroeder. Her husband had been killed in the shootout.

"He beat me to heaven," she later said.[3]

Her children were among those released from the compound immediately after the raid. Kathryn Schroeder left the compound on March 12. However, before she left, she witnessed the suicidal mood that Koresh was spreading among his followers.

Schroeder said that four days after the raid, Koresh began to instruct the Branch Davidians in how to commit mass suicide. One of Koresh's plans called for Schroeder to pull out the pin on a hand grenade in order to kill herself and four other women. Schroeder did not know if she would be able to do it.

"I was asking them, 'What are we going to do if I can't?'" she said. "And [the women] were reassuring me that I could."

Then Koresh called off the plan. He claimed he had seen another vision from God.

"God told David that we had all messed up," Schroeder said, "and if we had all died then, we would have gone to

Several children were released to outside authorities before the deadly fire. Asked to draw where she lived, one child even drew in the bullet holes in the compound's roof. She said the rainbow represented the kingdom of heaven.

*K*athryn Schroeder was sent out of the compound, along with other women and children. Federal agents held her in custody.

hell because of our sins after the raid." Koresh's list of so-called sins changed as often as his moods. This time, Koresh told the Davidians that their sins were drinking, smoking, and eating junk food. He was the one who sent Schroeder out of the compound, telling her he was displeased that she had been smoking cigarettes.[4]

Most of the negotiations for the Branch Davidians during the standoff were handled by Steve Schneider. He was considered Koresh's second-in-command. Schneider told FBI negotiators several times that he believed the FBI would eventually burn the compound. On March 27, 1993, the twenty-eighth day of the standoff, Schneider had this conversation with an FBI negotiator:

"Well, you know what I think would work—well, I better not say," Schneider said.

"Go ahead," replied the FBI negotiator.

"I was just going to say, throw a match to the building; people will have to come out," Schneider said.

"No, we're not going to do something like that," the negotiator told him.

"Sometime when you have a chance," Schneider said, "read Isaiah 33 about people living in fire and walking through it and coming out surviving."[5]

Koresh also predicted the standoff would end in fire, and he said the FBI and ATF would be responsible.

"You're going to smoke bomb us, or you're going to burn our building down," Koresh told negotiators shortly after the initial raid.[6]

The Branch-Davidian compound was indeed a fire hazard. Nearly every room had a gas lantern. Bales of hay had been brought in and stacked against some of the inside walls to serve as extra protection from gunfire from the outside. Gas lanterns and dry bales of hay were not a safe combination. One FBI negotiator recognized the hazard.

"Do you have any fire extinguisher systems?" the negotiator asked Steve Schneider. Schneider sent

*A*n unidentified Branch Davidian is taken away by authorities on April 4, after leaving the compound.

someone around the compound to count the number of fire extinguishers. He reported that they found only one.[7]

The standoff continued. During negotiations, Koresh repeatedly threatened that his group was ready to fight.

On April 18, FBI agents pulled all vehicles away from the area of the compound. Their tear-gas attack was set to begin the next morning.

As they cleared the area, an FBI sniper saw a cardboard sign decorated with images of fire in one of the windows.

Two words were written on it—"Flames Await."[8]

Fire and Ashes

At about 6 A.M. on April 19, 1993, the plan to end the fifty-one-day standoff went into action. FBI negotiators warned the Branch Davidians that they would be gassed if they did not come out of the compound immediately. When none of them came out, the armored vehicles moved toward the compound and began pumping the CS tear gas into the buildings. When the Branch Davidians began shooting at the armored vehicles, the four small Bradley tanks were brought in to deliver more gas, by firing tear gas canisters through the compound's windows. Six hours later, no one had come out.

Then, shortly after noon, the fire started. With the aid of gusty winds, the flames spread through the entire compound within minutes.

FBI agent Bob Ricks said that as the compound became engulfed in flames, "a man on the roof was spotted and signaled that he did not want to be rescued."[1]

*F*BI agent Bob Ricks (right) and ATF spokesman David Troy give a daily briefing on the Branch-Davidian situation.

At another part of the compound, a woman suddenly emerged from the blaze.

"A woman in flames was seen coming out of the compound and tried to run back into the building," said agent Ricks. "An FBI agent exited his armored vehicle, ran toward the building, and physically rescued the female despite her attempts to fight him off."[2]

A number of shots rang out inside the burning compound. At least seventeen of the Branch Davidians were killed by gunfire as the blaze closed in around them. Most of these gunshots were self-inflicted—suicides. A few, including the gunshots that killed two children, were inflicted by someone else.

One of these many gunshots ended the life of David Koresh. It is not known for certain whether Koresh committed suicide or if he was killed by someone else.

Most of the Branch Davidians who tried to make their way out of the fiery compound never escaped the flames. Unfortunately, the damage the armored vehicles inflicted to the compound's walls managed to hinder the Branch

Davidians' escape rather than aid it. Besides creating holes in the walls for the Davidians' escape, the tanks destroyed wooden stairways connecting the buildings' upper and lower floors, which left some members stranded in the burning upstairs portion of the compound.

The tanks also pushed debris over a trap door that opened to an underground passage. It was supposed to have served as an escape route to the outside. Six women made their way through the burning compound to the trap door. However, they found it blocked by fallen debris. The six women died of smoke inhalation within a few feet of the blocked door.

By 1 P.M., the Branch-Davidian compound, which had been intact only an hour earlier, was a smoldering ruin.

"We can only assume that there was a massive loss of life," Agent Ricks told the media. "It was truly an inferno of flames."[3]

Agent Ricks later read from a statement written by FBI director William Sessions. "I had hoped to report that today's careful and humane efforts by the FBI and ATF agents to bring the Branch Davidians out of their compound had resulted in a peaceful solution of the standoff." Ricks continued to read, "Instead, we are faced with destruction and death."[4]

The fiery destruction of the Branch-Davidian compound at Waco shocked Americans and people around the world. Yet despite the shocking way the standoff ended, the deaths of the Branch Davidians were not totally unexpected.

David Koresh and his followers had exhibited a number of erratic and dangerous behaviors. The Davidians believed that their leader could envision the end of the world. They believed in it, and they possessed a large and dangerous arsenal of weapons. This deadly combination had been seen before with other religious groups. So it was not completely surprising that an armed standoff with a group who believed in both guns and the end of the world would result in many of their deaths.

*T*he charred ruins of the Branch-Davidian compound. The swirls in the dirt were made by armored vehicles during the fifty-one-day standoff.

Some people responded to the fire at Waco with outrage. Many believed that the FBI and the ATF had been too aggressive in trying to end the siege with tanks and tear gas. Several antigovernment groups around the country thought that the FBI, either deliberately or by accident, had started the fire. Branch Davidians who survived the disaster claim that the FBI tanks crashed through the wall, knocking over gas lamps, which started the fire. However, conversations among Branch Davidians, recorded on tape by listening devices, suggest that Koresh and others in his group set the fire. Fire investigators found evidence of "pour patterns"—a distinctive kind of charring that occurs when gasoline, kerosene, or other fuels are used to ignite a fire. Several of these pour patterns were found inside the compound.

"That building was just saturated," a fire investigator said.[5]

Others have refuted the fire investigators' claims. A number of theories exist about how the fire was started and who actually ignited it. Because of the utter destruction to the compound and the small number of surviving witnesses, we will probably never know for certain who or what started the deadly blaze.

The FBI was also criticized for moving firefighting equipment away from the compound. Local fire departments did not receive their first reports of the fire until eight minutes after the blaze had begun. Even when local firefighters did arrive, the FBI kept them away from the burning building for almost thirty minutes.

Although both the FBI and the ATF were criticized for the way they handled the siege at Waco, they were also supported by many other people.

The fact that the tanks were repeatedly fired upon by the Branch Davidians may have been the reason for keeping the firefighters away. Authorities feared they might be shot by the Branch Davidians.

There is no doubt that mistakes were made by the ATF and the FBI during the raid and the long standoff that followed. Some critics have stated that the ATF should have arrested Koresh at a time when he was away from the Branch-Davidian compound. Such a move might have eliminated any possibility for a standoff. Overall, the ATF and FBI may have been too aggressive in how they dealt with Koresh and his followers. Lives might have been saved if the operation had been handled in a different way. But the problem these federal officers faced was not an easy one.

The Branch Davidians were heavily armed. They believed their leader, David Koresh, was a prophet. Koresh was prepared to fight, and many of his followers were prepared to follow him to their deaths. These factors combined to make a difficult and dangerous situation for law enforcement officials.

One reporter summed up the complexities of the situation: "The FBI's mistakes were procedural rather than fundamental. If its agents are truly guilty of anything, it is the guilt of those unable to prevent the inevitable."[6]

A number of FBI and ATF officials resigned after investigation and criticism of their handling of the Waco incident. It is still argued whether those who died amid

*I*n the aftermath, investigators dig for bodies of five Branch Davidians who were reportedly killed in the raid by federal agents on February 28, 1993.

the ashes were victims of governmental mistakes or of their own suicidal wishes.

Seventy-four people, including twenty-one children, were killed in the April 19 fire of the Branch-Davidian compound. Only nine Davidians survived.

At least seventeen of those found amid the ashes had been killed by gunfire. Most of them were found with bullet wounds in their heads. A few of the victims, including David Koresh, may have been shot by someone else.

FBI Agent Bob Ricks speculated that Koresh proved to be a fraud at the end. While his followers were dying around him, Ricks theorized, Koresh may have tried to escape the flames, but was instead shot by Schneider who would not tolerate Koresh's escape.[7]

Although Ricks's theory is an interesting one, it is just as likely that Koresh and Schneider planned a suicide pact, in which Schneider was to shoot Koresh before shooting himself.

The bodies of the Branch Davidians were not all that was found amid the ashes of the compound at Waco. Investigators found fifty-nine handguns, twelve shotguns, ninety-four rifles, and forty-five machine guns. The Branch Davidians' weapons stockpile included 1.8 million rounds of ammunition and a variety of hand-grenade parts. Perhaps the most lethal items among their arsenal were

*M*any of the bodies that were found in the ashes of Waco were stored and transported in this refrigeration truck.

Star High, age six, helps replace the crosses in an area dedicated to the people who died during the siege at Waco. Star's family, residents of Waco, had previously removed the crosses and cut the grass in honor of Mother's Day.

two powerful .50-caliber Barrett rifles, capable of hitting targets more than a mile away, and more than three dozen assault rifles.[8]

The disaster at Waco enraged militia groups around the United States who were already angry at the government for a wide range of reasons. Like Koresh and the Branch Davidians, these militia groups were always prepared to take up arms against the United States government.

On April 19, 1995, exactly two years after the Waco fire, the Alfred P. Murrah federal office building in Oklahoma City was bombed. Timothy McVeigh, who was found guilty of the bombing, was a member of a militia. McVeigh confessed he had bombed the federal office building as a way to lash out at the government for what had happened at Waco.

The disaster in Waco showed us that religious leaders who carry the Bible in one hand and a loaded gun in the other present a dangerous and difficult problem for our government—a problem that, in this case, ended in flames.

Chapter 1. A Sudden Inferno

1. Dick J. Reavis, "What Really Happened at Waco?" *Texas Monthly*, July 1995, p. 93.

2. Lee Hancock, "Koresh Trying to Provoke 'War,' Federal Officials Say," *The Dallas Morning News*, March 9, 1993, <http://www.dallasnews.com/waco/w0309b.html> (June 30, 1998).

3. Hancock, "Deadly Inferno: FBI Says Cult Torched Compound," *The Dallas Morning News*, April 20, 1993, <http://www.dallasnews.com/waco/w0420.html> (June 30, 1998).

4. Reavis, p. 94.

5. James D. Tabor and Eugene V. Gallagher, *Why Waco? Cults and the Battle for Religious Freedom in America* (Los Angeles: University of California Press, 1995), p. 2.

6. Reavis, p. 93.

7. Hancock, "Deadly Inferno: FBI Says Cult Torched Compound."

8. Ibid.

9. Reavis, p. 93.

10. Ibid.

11. Ibid.

Chapter 2. The Making of David Koresh

1. James A. Haught, *Holy Hatred: Religious Conflicts of the 90s* (New York: Prometheus Books, 1995), p. 212.

2. Ibid.

3. Jim McGee and William Claiborne, "The Transformation of the Waco 'Messiah,'" *The Washington Post*, May 9, 1993, p. A01.

4. Ibid.

5. Sue Anne Pressley, "Koresh 'Wife' Details Chaos in Waco Standoff," *The Washington Post*, February 3, 1994, p. A08.

6. McGee and Claiborne.

7. Howard Chua-Eoan, "Tripped Up by Lies," *Time*, October 11, 1993, p. 40.

8. Ibid.

Chapter 3. The Siege

1. James Popkin and Jeannye Thornton, "A Botched Mission in Waco, Texas," *U.S. News & World Report*, March 15, 1993, pp. 24–25.

2. Joan Biskupic and Pierre G. Thomas, "4 Agents Killed, 16 Hurt in Raid on Cult," *The Washington Post*, March 1, 1993, p. A01.

3. Sue Anne Pressley, "Koresh 'Wife' Details Chaos in Waco Standoff," *The Washington Post*, February 3, 1994, p. A08.

4. Ibid.

5. Dick J. Reavis, "What Really Happened at Waco?" *Texas Monthly*, July 1995, p. 91.

6. Ibid.

7. Ibid.

8. Lee Hancock, "Siege Chronology Reveals Frustrations, Disagreements," *The Dallas Morning News*, October 9, 1993, <http://www.dallasnews.com/waco/w1009.html> (January 1998).

Chapter 4. Fire and Ashes

1. Lee Hancock, "Deadly Inferno: FBI Says Cult Torched Compound," *The Dallas Morning News*, April 20, 1993, <http://www.dallasnews.com/waco/w0420.html> (June 30, 1998).

2. Ibid.

3. Ibid.

4. Ibid.

5. Lee Hancock, "FBI Agent Suggests Top Aide Killed Koresh," *The Dallas Morning News*, September 4, 1993, <http://www.dallasnews.com/waco/w0904.html> (June 30, 1998).

6. John Taylor, "The Waco Blame Game," *New York*, May 3, 1993, p. 12.

7. Hancock, "FBI Agent Suggests Top Aide Killed Koresh."

8. Gordon Witkin, "How David Koresh Got All Those Guns," *U.S. News & World Report*, June 7, 1993, p. 42.

Bureau of Alcohol, Tobacco, and Firearms (ATF)—The federal law enforcement agency responsible for investigating and making arrests involving the illegal sale and possession of weapons, alcohol, and cigarettes.

commune—A living arrangement in which a group of people share their home and resources.

Federal Bureau of Investigation (FBI)—The United States government agency in charge of investigating criminal activities within United States borders.

militia groups—Armed and organized groups of citizens who are prepared to take up weapons in an effort to combat what they perceive as oppression by the federal government.

Books

Gay, Kathlyn. *Militias: Armed and Dangerous.* Springfield, N.J.: Enslow Publishers, Inc., 1997.

Kronenwetter, Michael. *The FBI and Other Law Enforcement Agencies of the United States.* Springfield, N.J.: Enslow Publishers, Inc., 1997.

Smith, Richard and Sue I. Hamilton. *Wait-Out in Waco (Day of the Disaster).* Minneapolis: Abdo & Daughters, 1993.

Internet

Dallas Morning News. <http://www.dallasnews.com/specials/waco> (August 6, 1998).

Frontline Online. "Waco: The Inside Story." <http://www.pbs.org/wgbh/pages/frontline/waco/> (August 6, 1998).